CRAB

CRAB

BUYING • COOKING • CRACKING

ANDREA FRONCILLO & JENNIFER JEFFREY

TEN SPEED PRESS
Berkeley | Toronto

Ten Speed Press
PO Box 7123
Berkeley, California 94707
www.tenspeed.com

Distributed in Australia by Simon and Schuster Australia, in Canada by Ten Speed Press Canada, in New Zealand by Southern Publishers Group, in South Africa by Real Books, and in the United Kingdom and Europe by Publishers Group UK.

Cover and text design by Kate Basart/Union Pageworks
Food styling by Merilee Bordin
Prop styling by Leigh Noë
Food styling assistance by Nan Bullock and Alexa Hyman
Photography assistance by Justine Shockett

Library of Congress Cataloging-in-Publication Data
Froncillo, Andrea.
 Crab : buying, cooking, cracking / Andrea Froncillo and Jennifer Jeffrey.
    p. cm.
 Includes index.
 ISBN-10: 1-58008-860-0 (hardcover)
 ISBN-13: 978-1-58008-860-2 (hardcover)
 1. Cookery (Crabs) 2. Crabs. I. Jeffrey, Jennifer. II. Title.
 TX754.C83F76 2007
 641.6'95—dc22   2007010653

Printed in China

First printing, 2007

1 2 3 4 5 6 7 8 9 10 — 11 10 09 08 07

CONTENTS

A CRAB

PRIMER

It's a crabby world out there—more than four thousand unique crab species have been identi-fied; their names alone would fill a book. Fortunately, when we consider crab in a culinary context, the field narrows considerably. Though most crabs are considered to be edible, nearly every geographic region of the world has one favorite crab that usually winds up in the pot. Make that *pots*—thousands and thousands of pots! An estimated 1½ million tons of crab are consumed around the globe every single year. That's a lot of crab!

A CRAB IN EVERY POT

Depending on where on the planet you live, the crab on your plate might be slightly bigger or smaller; it might have black or white pincers; its shell might be brown or green or a rosy shade of pink; its meat might be more or less sweet—but no matter what it looks like, it will always taste like crab.

Here are some of most common edible crabs from around the world:

JAPANESE BLUE CRAB (*Portunus trituberculatus*), also known as HORSE CRAB, is harvested mainly off the coast of China. It is the most widely fished species of crab in the world, and can be found throughout Asia in hotpots and soups.

ALASKA SNOW CRAB (*Chionoecetes opilio*) is harvested from the cold waters of the Pacific and Atlantic Oceans. Called QUEEN CRAB in Canada, it is also known as SPIDER CRAB. This crab is often found on chain restaurant menus in the United States that serve crab legs as an entrée.

BLUE CRAB (*Callinectes sapidus*) is harvested in the Atlantic Ocean and the Gulf of Mexico, and is very popular on the East Coast of the United States.

MUD CRAB (*Scylla serrata*), also known as MANGROVE CRAB, is not found in the sea, but rather lives in the estuaries and mangroves of Africa, Australia, and Asia.

DUNGENESS CRAB (*Cancer magister*) is harvested in the cold waters of the Pacific Ocean from Alaska to as far south as Santa Barbara, California. It is the crab of choice for most chefs on the West Coast of the United States.

KING CRAB, despite its name, is not a crab at all, but a crab-like crustacean primarily found in cold seas. Most of the king crab in the U.S. market is imported from Russia.

SOFT-SHELL CRABS aren't a separate species of crab, but rather a stage in a crab's life. The hard shell of a crab prevents it from growing bigger; the only way it can grow is to molt. Every year, crabs cast off, or "molt," their entire shell. Before this happens, a new protective covering begins to form beneath the shell. When the shell is molted, the crab is soft and uncalcified. The crab grows rapidly in the space of a few days. When the new shell calcifies, the crab is again fixed at a certain size. Most soft-shell crabs on the U.S. market are blue crabs.

Other crabs you might find in your culinary explorations include PEEKEYTOE CRABS, STONE CRABS, and FLOWER CRABS. But if you're like most people, you are loyal to one species of crab and consider it to be better than all the rest.

CRAB CULTURE

On the East Coast of the United States, people are gung-ho for blue crab; they think it is the best crab in the world, and they don't mind saying so. Chesapeake Bay is famous for its blue crabs, so much so that Maryland's slogan is "Maryland is for crabs." Every year, this creature with brilliant blue pincers is celebrated at crab festivals all along the coastline, from Florida to South Carolina. If you take a drive through any of these coastal towns, you're likely to see countless signs advertising crabs, and many "crabby" slogans and folksy drawings designed to delight and amuse.

The West Coast of the United States is partial to Dungeness crab, which is harvested in the cold waters of the Pacific Ocean. Here in San Francisco, the Dungeness crab is one of the city's most popular icons, and people from all over the world flock to Fisherman's Wharf for a taste of this delicious creature. The Dungeness is renowned for its large size; most are between 1½ to 3 pounds, considerably larger than blue crabs, which makes their meat easier to extract. A single Dungeness crab is usually a good-sized meal for one person.

Elsewhere in the world, people are just as devoted to their local crabs. Residents of Hong Kong celebrate hairy crab season with relish; restaurants create entire menus around the crabs, while street vendors hawk baskets full of the live creatures to passersby. If you're traveling in Samoa, Fiji, or northern Australia, you're likely to find a piquant mud crab stew on the menu. If you ever have the occasion to conduct a business deal in Indonesia, don't be surprised if dinner involves rolling up your sleeves and cracking through a crab slathered in spicy chile sauce.

If you're crazy for crab, you not only have lots of company, but you're also sure to find a crab to fill your craving—almost anywhere you look!

CRAB IN SAN FRANCISCO

Chef Andrea Froncillo has been cooking with crab for many years. He grew up in the seaside town of Napoli, Italy, where the local crab was tossed into pasta dishes or made into crab cakes. When he moved to San Francisco in 1979, he immediately began experimenting with Dungeness crab. Today, Andrea and his partners own two restaurants on Fisherman's Wharf, the Crab House on Pier 39 and the Franciscan Crab House on Pier 43½.

When the two of us, Andrea and food writer Jennifer Jeffrey, sat down to begin this cookbook, we discussed the fact that many people eat crab at restaurants, but are hesitant to cook with it at home. We decided to assemble a collection of crab recipes that are not only delicious, but also uncomplicated and easy to make. Some of the recipes in this cookbook are adaptations of favorite menu items from Andrea's restaurants, while others are new creations. We hope you'll have as much fun as we did cooking with crab!

Since we're writing from San Francisco, our crab of choice is the Dungeness. We love its hefty size and its sweet, silky meat. Even better, we love that the Monterey Bay Aquarium, which has created a Seafood Watch program and publishes a guide to sustainable seafood, has given the Dungeness crab its "best" rating, which means it is an abundant, sustainable resource and can be enjoyed without harming the environment. That means that we can indulge in one of our favorite treats as often as we please. Since crab is equally delicious for breakfast, lunch, and dinner, that means we eat it often! We've included recipes for all courses in this book, so you'll be able to enjoy crab any time you get a hankering for it.

Fisherman's Wharf in San Francisco is the historic site where fishermen brought their sailboats during the Gold Rush and braved the fog to bring in their catch. Many of those first sailors were Italian immigrants from Sicily and Calabrese, and it is said that the misty air was filled with the sailors' renditions of Verdi as they sailed back and forth. The popular Italian fish stew *zuppa de pesce* (or as it's known in northern Italy, *cacciucco*) became "cioppino" in San Francisco when Dungeness crab was added to it. Dungeness crab was and still is a celebrated catch for local fishermen. Throughout the year, seafood stalls around the Wharf sell freshly steamed crab, crab cakes, and crab chowder for the passersby, while local restaurants offer a wealth of crab dishes, from crab cakes to crab pizza. The gorgeous old sign marking the entrance to the Wharf features a Dungeness crab at its center, and when crab season opens each November, the Wharf has a party! The cauldrons alongside the Wharf are lighted, and the boats begin to arrive, loaded with the inaugural catch of these beautiful crimson-colored creatures.

It is possible to purchase freshly harvested Dungeness crabs at West Coast fish markets nearly all year round. Dungeness crab is a cyclical resource, and fishermen harvest it up and down the Pacific Coast, starting in California in November and ending in Alaska in the summer and early fall. There are only three weeks of the year when fresh Dungeness is not available; during three weeks in September, all areas are closed to commercial fishing.

HOW TO USE THIS COOKBOOK

Most of the recipes in this book were developed using Dungeness crab; however, if you live in other parts of the country, feel free to substitute blue crab or other local crabmeat. Keep in mind that smaller crabs may take slightly less time to cook. We've included either a weight (in ounces) or volume measurement in every recipe that calls for crabmeat; if you are extracting the meat yourself, the size of the crab you use doesn't matter as long as you have the amount of crabmeat the recipe calls for.

Recipes such as salads, where the crabmeat is not mixed into other ingredients, should be made with fresh crabmeat. These recipes clearly specify "fresh crabmeat." Other recipes, such as soups and baked dishes, can be made with different types and grades of crabmeat. In these recipes, we've simply indicated "crabmeat." You can use fresh, canned, or frozen crabmeat in these dishes. Whatever type of crabmeat you choose, you will benefit from choosing the highest grade of crabmeat possible for the optimum flavor and texture.

Crab is simple to buy and prepare. Don't let the how-to's intimidate you; as soon as you get started, you'll discover how easy it is to work with crab.

HOW TO PURCHASE CRAB

When you purchase live or cooked crabs, be sure to shop at a reputable market or fishmonger in order to get the best-quality product. Look for live crabs that are active and feisty; avoid ones that are sluggish or still.

While most blue crabs on the East Coast are sold live, most Dungeness crabs on the West Coast are sold pre-cooked. If you're purchasing whole cooked crabs, ask the person at the fish counter to help you pick out the best specimen. In general, the bigger crabs are better; the front legs are where most of the good meat resides, while the back legs contain small bits of meat that are hard to pick out. Pre-cooked crabs must still be cleaned before you use them in a recipe.

Fresh soft-shell crabs are available from late spring to early fall and should always be purchased live, not cooked, to ensure the best flavor and texture; during other parts of the year, they can be can be purchased frozen. Look for live soft-shell crabs with a stream of bubbles coming from their mouth. The "shell" should be transparent and soft—the softer, the better. Avoid crabs with a rough, papery shell. Medium-sized soft-shell crabs are generally sweeter and more tender than the larger ones.

We recommend that you use fresh crabmeat from your local fish market whenever possible for the best flavor and texture; it's available several months of the year, depending upon where you live. If you can't find fresh crabmeat, look for frozen or canned varieties. Don't shy away from frozen crabmeat; if you buy from a reputable source, it was likely blast-frozen at the peak of freshness, and is therefore high quality.

While fresh crabmeat is the optimal choice, canned crabmeat can be used in its place. Canned crabmeat is generally softer in texture, and slightly less expensive than its fresh counterpart. Canned crabmeat is sold by grade, based on the sizes of the pieces and their texture.

JUMBO LUMP CRABMEAT is the highest grade and most expensive canned crabmeat on the market. These beautiful "lumps" of crabmeat are best used in salads and other preparations where the crabmeat adorns the top of a dish and won't get lost in a sauce.

BACKFIN AND SPECIAL CRABMEAT consist of smaller chunks and flakes of crabmeat. Both backfin and special crabmeat have terrific flavor, and are perfect in recipes like crab cakes, baked crab dishes, or crab pastas. They can also be used in soups and chowders, or in preparations where the appearance of the crab isn't important.

CLAW MEAT is the crab equivalent of dark meat in poultry and has a slightly stronger flavor than the other parts of the crab. It can be mixed with other crabmeat as an "extender," or it can be used alone in sauces, dips, and soups.

Whether you choose live, cooked, canned, or frozen crab, let your nose have the final say on freshness. Crab should smell fresh and slightly salty, with a faint whiff of seawater. Discard crab that smells sour or overly fishy, or gives off an odor of ammonia.

Before using crabmeat in a recipe, pick through the meat with a seafood fork or your fingers to find and remove any tiny bits of shell.

HOW TO STORE CRAB

Live crabs should be cooked and eaten within 12 hours of purchase. Until you are ready to cook them, place them in a deep dish and cover with damp paper towels. Store in the refrigerator. Do not store them in an airtight container or in a container filled with water, or they will die.

Fresh crabmeat can be stored for 2 to 3 days in the refrigerator in a tightly sealed container. Frozen crabmeat can be kept in the freezer for up to 6 months, as long as it is tightly sealed to prevent freezer burn. Some canned crabmeat must be refrigerated, while some can be stored at room temperature until opened; follow the guidelines on the can or jar that indicate where it should be stored, and be sure to note the expiration date.

HOW TO CLEAN AND PREPARE CRAB

Many of the recipes in this book call for crabmeat. You can either buy crabmeat in various forms, or you can buy whole live or cooked crabs and extract the meat yourself.

Better yet, you may want to have a crab feast by buying live crabs and boiling or roasting them to crack and eat directly from the shell. East Coasters often make a party of it, lining a dining table or picnic table with newspapers and throwing down whole steamed crabs directly from the pot to be cracked and eaten with drawn butter.

Whatever you plan to do with your crab, here is how to get started:

KILLING LIVE CRABS. Do not plunge live crabs directly into boiling water. Not only does this cause the creatures to suffer, but it also makes the meat tough. Killing a crab is easily accomplished with a pair of kitchen shears or a clean screwdriver. Use caution when handling live crabs; they will not hesitate to make use of their pincers! If you can, refrigerate the crabs for at least 1 hour before handling them; the cold temperature makes them sluggish, and therefore easier to handle. Most live crabs purchased from a market have rubber bands wrapped around their pincers; don't remove these bands until after the crab is dead! Turn the crab on to its back so that the legs are pointing up. Insert the screwdriver or the closed point of the scissors into the mouth and drive it forward and up, right between the eyes, until it hits the other side of the shell. Turn the crab back over and allow it to drain for about 20 seconds.

CLEANING RAW AND COOKED CRABS. You can clean a crab before or after cooking it, but we recommend that you do it beforehand. It is much easier to clean a cold crab than a hot one, and far less messy.

1. Pull off the top shell. Rinse the shell and reserve it if you want to use it to decorate or serve your dish.

2. Turn the crab over and place your thumb in the middle of the triangular-shaped breast-plate, watching out for the soft spines beneath it. Remove and discard the breastplate and spines. With your thumb, scrape away and discard the white leaf-like gills on the underside of the body. Remove the crab "butter," the soft white and yellow intestinal mass in the center of the body cavity. Many cultures consider crab butter a delicacy, and many chefs add it to crab dishes to enhance the crab flavor. Reserve the butter if you want to use it in your recipe. Rinse out the body cavity under cold running water.

    If you're going to cook the crab whole, you're finished! If you're going to break the crab into individual legs to be cooked, or if you want to extract the meat from a cooked crab for a recipe, move on to step 3.

3. Grasp the crab by the middle and break the body into two equal halves.

4. Break off the legs from each half, one by one. You're now ready to roast the legs or, if the crab is already cooked, you may now crack your crab and eat it, or extract the meat to use in your recipe of choice.

    Crack the crab using crab crackers; in a pinch, you can use a nutcracker. Hold the crab leg and gently crack across the seam to break the shell. Avoid using a mallet or other heavy instrument to crack crab, as the meat is very delicate and easily smashed. Use seafood forks or crab picks to extract the meat. Enjoy!

COOKING WHOLE CRABS. Bring a large pot of salted water to a boil over high heat. Kill and clean the crabs (see page 21) and plunge them into the water. Cook for 18 to 20 minutes, until they turn bright red. Using tongs, remove the crabs from the water and pat dry. Serve immediately. If you are going to extract the meat to use in a recipe, cool the crabs before handling by plunging them into a basin of cold water for 3 to 4 minutes.

HEATING PRE-COOKED CRABS. Clean the crabs first, then bring a large pot of salted water to a boil over high heat. Plunge the crabs into the water for about 1 minute to heat through. Remove and pat dry. Serve immediately.

1.

2.

3.

4.

With their whimsical shape and luxurious flavor, crabs are a festive dish. Many of the recipes you'll find in this book are perfect for parties, special occasions, or holiday celebrations. If you're making a crab dish that involves whole crab or crab legs and claws, you'll want to have the necessary implements on hand to ensure that your dinner guests enjoy their meal to its fullest!

Here's what we recommend you have on hand when you're serving crab:

BIBS. Eating crab is a messy affair! Just pull out the bibs at the start of a meal, and you won't have to worry about staining your favorite shirt. Not only is it practical, but for what other occasion can you gracefully wear a bib?

BOWLS FOR SHELLS. For quick, easy cleanup, put a couple of empty bowls on the table for empty crab shells.

WARM, MOIST TOWELS. Fingers can get slippery from cracking crab and dipping the pieces into butter. Before a crab feast, dip hand towels into a basin of clean water, wring out excess water, roll the towels up, and place them on a microwave-safe platter. As the meal draws to an end, pop the platter into a microwave for 30 to 45 seconds. Remove and pass around the table; the warm towels will cure buttery fingers in an instant!

LEMON WEDGES. Some people complain that their hands smell "crabby" after a crab meal. To eliminate unwanted odors, pass around a dish of freshly cut lemon wedges for guests to rub on their hands. Let hands air-dry for instant odor removal!

FINGER BOWLS. If you don't have a microwave to warm up hand towels, you can set finger bowls on the table instead. Place shallow bowls of lukewarm water at each setting, and float thin slices of lemon on the top of the water. Your guests can rinse their crabby fingers in the bowl and pat them dry on clean napkins.

CRAB CRACKERS. Most fish markets and kitchen goods stores carry crab crackers. We like the stainless-steel ones, which are much more durable than the plastic sort. In a pinch, you can use a nutcracker. Remember, when using crab crackers: crack, don't smash! You don't want to damage the delicate meat inside the shell. For this reason, we don't recommend that you use any kind of mallet or hammer to crack crab shells; doing so will bruise the meat and cause the flavorful chunks of meat to separate into flakes.

SEAFOOD FORKS OR CRAB PICKS. Once a crab has been cracked, the shell can be gently pulled apart to reveal the meat inside. Some of the pieces will be easy to remove with your fingers; other bits of meat might need to be teased out with the help of a seafood fork or a crab pick. These implements are small enough to wedge into the small crevices near the joints, where you can often find wonderful pieces of meat. Seafood forks and crab picks can be found at fish markets or cookware stores.

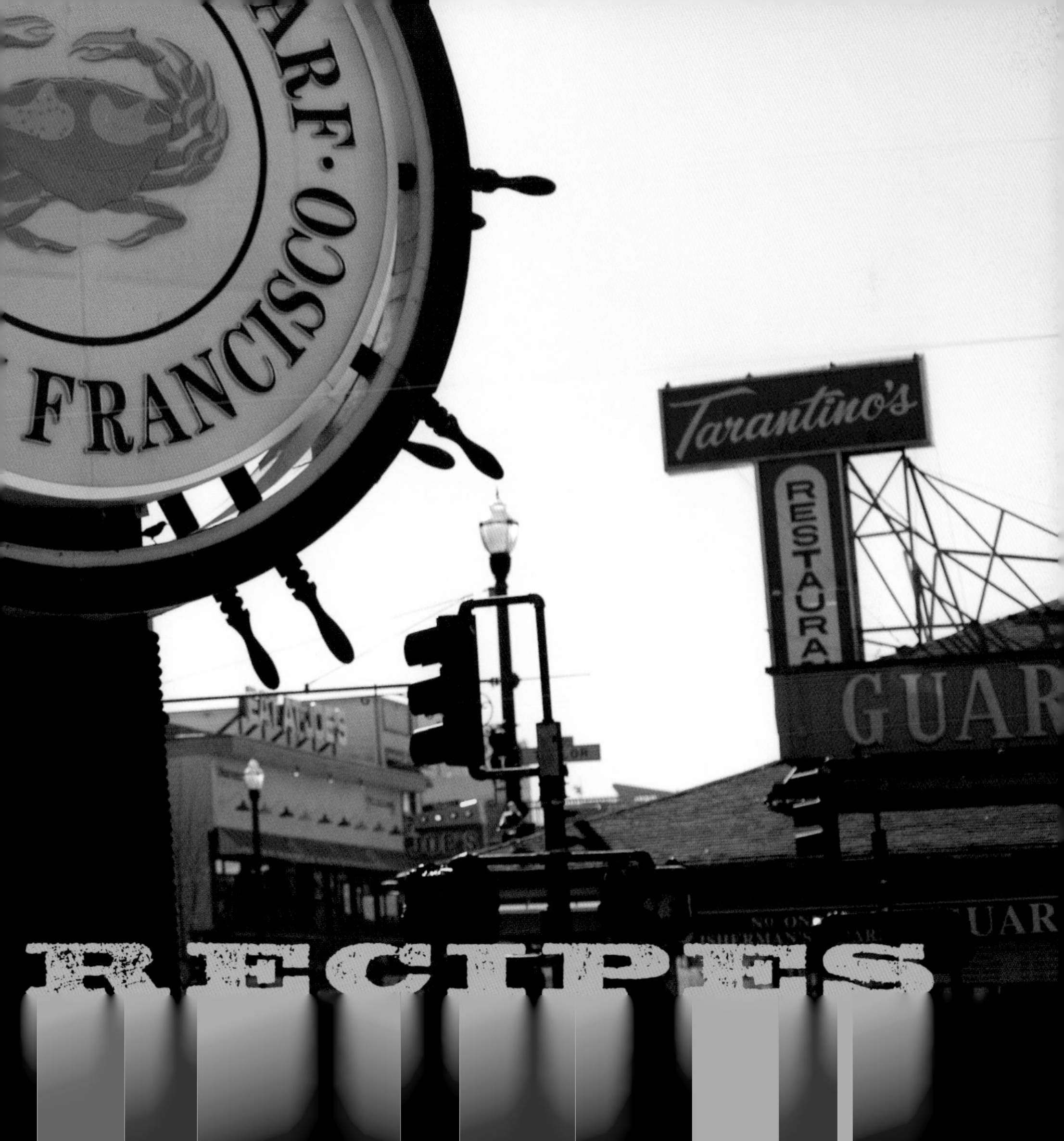

RECIPES

SOUPS

CRAB GAZPACHO

When we think of gazpacho, we think of a refreshing repast on a hot summer day. Gazpacho has been called "liquid salad," as it is essentially a chilled puree of raw vegetables. Over the years, gazpacho has taken on many forms, and we believe that crab makes it even better. Use the freshest ingredients you can find—tomatoes at their peak of ripeness really make the flavors sing. If you plan to make this soup more than 2 hours ahead of serving, don't add the jalapeño, as its heat can become too intense after standing for 3 or 4 hours.

2½ pounds ripe tomatoes
1 cucumber, peeled, seeded, and quartered
⅓ cup firmly packed fresh flat-leaf parsley leaves
3 tablespoons minced fresh cilantro
1 cup tomato juice, plus 1 tablespoon
½ cup red wine vinegar
3 tablespoons extra-virgin olive oil
3 garlic cloves, minced
1 jalapeño pepper, seeded and minced
2 teaspoons salt
½ teaspoon freshly ground black pepper
6 ounces fresh crabmeat (¾ cup)
2 tablespoons diced green onion
1 tablespoon freshly squeezed lime juice
1 avocado, peeled, pitted, and diced

- To peel and seed the tomatoes, score the bottoms of the tomatoes with an X. In a pot of salted boiling water, blanch 2 or 3 tomatoes at a time for 30 to 60 seconds, until the skins begin to peel back where scored. Using a wire-mesh skimmer, transfer to a bowl of cold water. Quickly peel the tomatoes. Repeat with the remaining tomatoes. Cut the tomatoes in half and gently squeeze or scrape out the seeds.

- In a food processor, puree the cucumber until almost smooth, with only a few small chunks remaining. Pour into a large bowl. In the food processor, puree the tomatoes until smooth. Pour into the bowl with the cucumber. In the food processor, process the parsley until minced. Add to the bowl with the tomatoes and cucumber.

- Add the cilantro, the 1 cup tomato juice, the vinegar, olive oil, garlic, jalapeño, salt, and pepper to the tomato mixture. Stir to combine. Cover and refrigerate for 1 to 2 hours to chill thoroughly and allow the flavors to meld.

- Just before serving, combine the crabmeat, green onions, lime juice, and the remaining 1 tablespoon tomato juice in a small bowl. Divide the gazpacho among 4 chilled soup bowls and place a scoop of the crab mixture in each. Sprinkle with the avocado. Serve immediately.

Serves 4 as a first course

CIOPPINO

This hearty fish stew is one of our favorite dishes for fall and winter—bring a loaf of hot, crusty bread to the table, and dinner is served! Be sure to pass crab crackers and warm hand towels.

4 tablespoons olive oil

3 tablespoons chopped fennel (reserve fennel fronds)

3 tablespoons chopped yellow onion

3 tablespoons minced shallots

3 garlic cloves, minced

¼ cup dry white wine

1 (28-ounce) can crushed tomatoes

2 tablespoons minced fresh flat-leaf parsley

1 teaspoon red pepper flakes

1 cup bottled clam juice

1 cup water

Salt and freshly ground black pepper

½ cup (1 stick) unsalted butter

1 pound P.E.I. (Prince Edward Island) mussels

8 ounces Manila or littleneck clams, scrubbed

8 ounces Dungeness crab legs in the shell

1 (8-ounce) white fish fillet (such as halibut, cod, or tilapia), cut into chunks

6 ounces large (21 to 30 per pound) shrimp, shelled and deveined

2 tablespoons minced fresh basil

- In a large, heavy saucepan, heat 2 tablespoons of the olive oil over medium-low heat. Add the chopped fennel, onion, shallots, and garlic and sauté for 7 to 8 minutes, until golden brown. Stir in the wine, then the tomatoes, parsley, pepper flakes, clam juice, water, and salt, and pepper to taste. Bring to a boil over high heat, then decrease the heat to low, cover, and simmer for 30 minutes. Add the butter and stir to melt. Remove from the heat.

- In a large, cast-iron skillet, heat the remaining 2 tablespoons olive oil over medium heat and toss in the mussels and clams. Cook, uncovered, for 4 minutes. As the mussels and clams begin to open, add the crab legs, fillet, and shrimp and sprinkle with salt and pepper to taste. Sauté for 2 to 3 minutes, until the shrimp turn pink. Discard any mussels or clams that do not open. Add 1 cup of the tomato mixture; bring to a simmer and cook for 5 minutes. Transfer the contents of the skillet to the saucepan with the remaining tomato mixture and simmer for 2 to 3 minutes.

- Ladle into soup bowls. Sprinkle with basil, garnish with the reserved fennel fronds, and serve.

Serves 4 to 6 as a main course

CRAB CHOWDER

IN A SOURDOUGH BREAD BOWL

If you've ever taken a stroll along Fisherman's Wharf, you know that one of the treats you'll find there is sourdough bread bowls brimming with seafood chowder. We've made our chowder with crab, bacon, and potatoes, creating a hearty and satisfying meal. The combination of tangy sourdough, one of San Francisco's specialties, and piping hot soup is perfect for a cool, foggy day, no matter where in the world you are.

1 cup diced apple wood–smoked bacon

½ cup diced celery

½ cup diced carrot

¼ cup diced red bell pepper

¼ cup diced yellow bell pepper

½ cup diced yellow onion

⅓ cup dry white wine

2 cups bottled clam juice

1 cup water

3 cups peeled diced russet potatoes

2 cups fresh or frozen corn kernels

1 tablespoon minced fresh thyme

1 tablespoon minced fresh flat-leaf parsley

1 tablespoon minced fresh tarragon

¼ teaspoon cayenne pepper

1 teaspoon salt, plus more as needed

1 teaspoon freshly ground black pepper, plus more as needed

1 cup heavy cream

continued on page 36

1 large round sourdough loaf, or 4 miniature round sourdough loaves

6 ounces canned jumbo lump crabmeat (¾ cup)

2 tablespoons freshly squeezed lemon juice

2 tablespoons thinly sliced green onions for garnish

1 tablespoon extra-virgin olive oil for garnish

- In a large, heavy pot, sauté the bacon over medium heat for 5 to 7 minutes, until the edges are browned and crisp. Remove from the heat and drain off the fat, leaving the bacon in the pot. Return to medium heat and add the diced vegetables. Sauté for 10 minutes, or until the celery and onion are soft and the carrots and peppers have softened.

- Add the wine and stir to scrape up the browned bits from the bottom of the pan. Add the clam juice, water, diced potatoes, and corn. Add the thyme, parsley, tarragon, cayenne, the 1 teaspoon salt, and the 1 teaspoon black pepper. Cover and simmer over medium-low heat for 30 to 45 minutes, until the potatoes are soft and the chowder has begun to thicken. Stir in the cream and continue to simmer for 5 more minutes.

- Preheat the broiler. Cut the top (about a 4-inch round) off of the sourdough loaf and scoop out the bread in the center, leaving a wall of bread about ½ inch thick on all sides. Put the loaf on a baking sheet and place under the broiler about 6 to 10 inches from the heat source for about 4 minutes, or until the bread on the inside of the loaf is crisp and just barely golden.

- In a small bowl, combine the crab and lemon juice. Season to taste with salt and pepper. Add to the chowder. Remove the loaf from the oven and place on a serving platter. Ladle hot chowder inside the loaf. Garnish with the green onions and a few drops of olive oil. Serve immediately.

Serves 4 to 6 as a first course

CRAB BISQUE

Crab has a wonderful chameleonlike quality: It is equally at home in rustic dishes and elegant preparations. In this stylish recipe, we create a richly flavored stock by boiling crab shells with water and wine. The resulting bisque is intense but light—a sophisticated starter that is perfectly suited to delicate china bowls.

2 large (2 pounds each) live or pre-cooked Dungeness crabs, or 4 or 5 large live or pre-cooked blue crabs

5 cups water

2 cups dry white wine

2 cups fish stock

1 cup beef stock

6 tablespoons unsalted butter

1 cup diced yellow onion

1 cup diced carrot

¼ cup finely chopped celery

8 to 10 large tomatoes, peeled (see page 31), seeded, and chopped (1½ cups)

⅓ cup long-grain white rice

1 bay leaf

1½ teaspoons minced fresh tarragon

½ teaspoon sweet paprika

1 teaspoon minced garlic

1 teaspoon salt, plus more as needed

½ teaspoon minced fresh thyme

1 teaspoon freshly ground black pepper, plus more as needed

½ cup Cognac or brandy

1 cup heavy cream

continued on page 38

- If you are using live crabs, kill and clean the crabs according to the directions on page 21. In a large, heavy pot, combine the water, wine, fish stock, and beef stock. Bring to a simmer over high heat. Put the crabs in the pot, back side down, and boil for about 10 minutes, or until the crabs are pink all over and the claws turn red. A stream of foam may rise from the head area of the crabs as they heat up; this is normal. Using tongs, remove the crabs from the pot and plunge into a basin of cold water for 3 to 4 minutes to cool. Skim the foam from the broth and reduce the heat to low. Using a crab cracker, crack the crab claws, legs, and body. Using a seafood fork or a crab pick, extract all of the crabmeat. Put the meat in a bowl and set aside. Return the empty shells to the pot.

- If you are using pre-cooked crabs, clean the crabs as described on page 22. Using a crab cracker, crack the crab claws, legs, and body. Using a seafood fork or a crab pick, extract all of the crabmeat. Put the meat in a small bowl; set aside. Add the empty shells to the broth. Bring to a simmer over high heat.

- Simmer the broth with the crab shells, uncovered, for 30 to 40 minutes, until the broth has reduced to about half of its original volume. You should have about 6 cups of liquid remaining. If you have less, add water to make up the difference. Remove from the heat and strain through a fine-meshed sieve. Discard the solids; return the strained broth to the pot.

- In a skillet, melt 3 tablespoons of the butter over medium heat. Add the onion, carrot, and celery. Sauté for 7 to 10 minutes, until the onions are soft and the celery and carrots have begun to soften.

- Add the sautéed vegetables to the broth along with the tomatoes, rice, bay leaf, tarragon, paprika, garlic, the 1 teaspoon salt, the thyme, and the 1 teaspoon pepper. Bring to a boil, reduce the heat to low, cover, and simmer for 15 minutes.

- In the skillet, melt the remaining 3 tablespoons butter. Add the Cognac and salt and pepper to taste. Add all but 2 to 3 tablespoons of the crabmeat, reserving the rest for garnish. Cook just until the liquid has evaporated, about 5 minutes. Add the crabmeat to the soup.

- With a slotted spoon, remove the bay leaf from the soup. In a food processor or blender, puree the soup in batches. Return to the pot and add the cream, stirring to combine. Place the pot over low heat for about 5 minutes, or until heated through. Divide among warmed soup bowls and garnish with the reserved crabmeat. Serve.

Serves 4 to 6 as a first course

HOT & SOUR CRAB SOUP

This vibrantly colored soup delivers both tangy and sour flavors that tease the palate and highlight crab in an intriguing way.

1 cup diced peeled tart apples, such as Granny Smith

1 cup diced peeled beets

1 cup thinly sliced yellow onion

2 teaspoons sea salt

1 teaspoon freshly ground black pepper

2 tablespoons unsalted butter, cut into ½-inch chunks

10 cups water

6 to 8 asparagus stalks, trimmed and cut into 2-inch diagonal slices (½ cup)

½ cup sliced green onions, including green parts

1 tablespoon dry mustard mixed with 2 tablespoons water

2 tablespoons minced shallots

2 tablespoons rice vinegar

3 tablespoons soy sauce

2 tablespoons yellow miso

8 ounces crabmeat (1 cup)

■ Preheat the oven to 350°F. Generously butter a 9 by 13-inch baking dish. In a bowl, combine the apples, beets, onion, 1 teaspoon of the salt, and the pepper. Stir in the butter. Pour into the prepared dish and bake, stirring once or twice, for 30 minutes, or until the vegetables are softened and beginning to turn golden brown around the edges.

- In a large, heavy pot, combine the water, the remaining 1 teaspoon salt, the asparagus, and the green onions. Add the mustard mixture, shallots, vinegar, soy sauce, and miso. Bring to a boil, then reduce the heat to medium-low. Add the roasted vegetables and simmer for 10 to 15 minutes, until the flavors are combined. Remove from the heat and add the crabmeat. Ladle into warmed soup bowls and serve.

Serves 4 to 6 as a first course

SALADS

CRAB LOUIS

Crab Louis (pronounced Louie) is one of the most requested crab dishes on the West Coast. There is debate as to its provenance—some claim that it originated in Seattle, while others say that a chef in San Francisco first brought this salad to the table—but everyone agrees that the "king of salads" is the ideal way to enjoy fresh crabmeat.

1 cup mayonnaise

¼ cup ketchup

2 tablespoons pickle relish

1 teaspoon prepared horseradish

2 tablespoons freshly squeezed lemon juice

1 teaspoon freshly ground pepper

4 teaspoons capers, ground to a chunky paste in a mortar or mashed with a fork

2 heads butter lettuce

1½ pounds fresh crabmeat (3 cups), chilled

4 hard-cooked eggs, sliced into quarters

2 lemons, each cut into 4 wedges

Capers for garnish

- In a small bowl, combine the mayonnaise, ketchup, relish, horseradish, lemon juice, pepper, and capers. Whisk until creamy.

- With a paring knife, carefully remove the core from the butter lettuce and open the head, keeping the leaves intact. Divide each head in half. Fan out the leaves of each half on a salad plate. Mound the crabmeat in the center of each lettuce fan. Arrange 4 egg quarters and 2 lemon wedges on opposite sides of each plate and garnish each salad with a sprinkling of capers. Pass the dressing on the side. Serve immediately.

Serves 4 as a first course or light lunch

FOGGY WHARF SALAD

This recipe is named for the fog that rolls in every afternoon off San Francisco Bay. It's a fresh mix of salad ingredients, crispy fried wonton strips, and sesame seeds, tossed in a tart-sweet dressing that perfectly accents the crab. The combination of bright colors makes it an attractive addition to the table.

> ¼ cup rice vinegar
> 1 tablespoon sugar
> 1 teaspoon minced fresh ginger
> 2 tablespoons toasted sesame oil
> ¼ cup low-sodium soy sauce
> 10 to 12 (4-inch) round wonton wrappers
> Canola oil for deep-frying
> 4 cups mixed baby greens
> 1 cup cherry tomatoes
> Salt and freshly ground black pepper
> 8 ounces fresh crabmeat (1 cup)
> 3 tablespoons black sesame seeds

- In a small bowl, whisk together the vinegar, sugar, ginger, sesame oil, and soy sauce. Set aside.

- Stack the wonton wrappers on a cutting board and cut them into matchsticks. In a large, heavy skillet, heat 1 to 2 inches canola oil over high heat to 375°F; the oil should be hot and bubbly. Scatter the strips into the oil, several at a time. Fry for 30 seconds to 1 minute, until the strips curl and become golden brown and crisp. Using a slotted spoon, transfer to paper towels to drain.

continued on page 48

■ In a large bowl, gently toss together the baby greens, cherry tomatoes, and all but a few wonton strips. Pour the dressing over the top and toss again. Season to taste with salt and pepper. Divide among serving plates and arrange the crabmeat on top. Sprinkle with the sesame seeds and the remaining wonton strips. Serve immediately.

Serves 4 as a first course or light lunch

CRAB & FUJI APPLE SALAD

WITH RASPBERRY VINAIGRETTE

This beautiful salad is tossed with a sweet-tart vinaigrette and crowned with crabmeat for a mix of flavors that is at once refreshing and extravagant. The candied walnuts offer a satisfying crunch; you may want to substitute pecans or hazelnuts, which can be prepared the same way.

8 ounces fresh crabmeat

1 tablespoon olive oil

1 teaspoon sea salt

1 teaspoon freshly ground black pepper

½ cup walnut halves

1 tablespoon unsalted butter

2 tablespoons packed brown sugar

¼ cup fresh raspberries

¼ cup raspberry vinegar

2 tablespoons granulated sugar

¼ cup water

4 cups mixed baby greens

1 cup torn romaine hearts

1 large Fuji apple, peeled, cored, sliced, and tossed with 1 teaspoon freshly squeezed lemon juice

continued on page 50

- In a small bowl, combine the crabmeat, oil, salt, and pepper. Toss lightly to coat. Set aside.

- In a medium, dry skillet over medium heat, toast the walnuts for 4 to 5 minutes, until slightly browned and fragrant. Watch carefully so that they don't burn. Remove from the heat and empty into a bowl to cool.

- In a small skillet, melt the butter over medium heat. Add the brown sugar and stir to combine. Add the walnuts; toss to coat thoroughly. Cook for 3 to 4 minutes, until the sugar begins to caramelize around the walnuts. Remove from the heat and spread in a single layer on a sheet of parchment paper. The sugar will harden around the walnuts.

- To prepare the raspberry vinaigrette, thoroughly mash the raspberries in a small bowl. Using a large spoon, press through a fine-meshed sieve to remove the seeds. In a small jar, combine the vinegar, granulated sugar, water, and raspberry puree. Seal and shake thoroughly until all the ingredients are blended.

- In a salad bowl, toss the baby greens and romaine together. Add the apple slices and candied walnuts. Drizzle with half of the vinaigrette and toss, using more vinaigrette if desired.

- Divide among serving plates and top with the crabmeat mixture. Serve immediately.

Serves 4 to 6 as a first course

THAI-STYLE SOFT-SHELL CRAB SALAD

Soft-shell blue crabs are harvested in the few short days between the time the crabs shed their old shell and grow a new one. In this "molting" stage, crabs have thin, papery husks that lend them perfectly to being lightly battered and fried. We've paired these crunchy creatures with Thai-inspired salad ingredients for a delectably delicious dish.

6 soft-shell crabs

1 egg

1 tablespoon water

1 cup rice flour

1 cup all-purpose flour

1 tablespoon sugar

2 teaspoons salt

1 teaspoon freshly ground black pepper

1 teaspoon red chile powder

Canola oil for deep-frying

¼ cup olive or canola oil

3 tablespoons rice vinegar

2 tablespoons fish sauce

1 tablespoon sugar

1 teaspoon red pepper flakes

Juice of ½ lime

1 teaspoon freshly ground black pepper

4 cups mixed baby greens

1 bunch cilantro, stemmed and coarsely chopped

continued on page 52

1 cucumber, thinly sliced

½ red onion, thinly sliced

1 red bell pepper, seeded, deveined, and cut into strips

½ cup dry-roasted peanuts

■ Pat the crabs dry with a paper towel. In a shallow bowl, beat the egg with the water. In another shallow bowl, combine the rice flour, all-purpose flour, sugar, salt, pepper, and chile powder.

■ In a large, heavy skillet, heat 1 to 2 inches oil over high heat to 375°F; it should be hot and bubbly. Dip one crab at a time into the egg wash, then dredge it in the seasoned flour until thoroughly coated, lightly tapping it against the side of the bowl to remove any excess. Using a wire-mesh skimmer, lower the crab into the oil and fry for about 2 minutes, until golden brown and crisp all over. Transfer to paper towels to drain; move to a plate and keep warm in a low oven while frying the remaining crabs. Repeat with the remaining crabs.

■ In a small bowl, combine the olive oil, vinegar, fish sauce, sugar, red pepper flakes, lime juice, and pepper. Whisk until blended. In a large bowl, combine the mixed greens, cilantro, cucumber, red onion, and bell pepper, tossing to mix. Drizzle the dressing over the salad and toss to coat.

■ Using tongs, place a generous heap of salad on each serving plate. Sprinkle with peanuts and place one of the fried crabs on top. Serve immediately.

Serves 6 as a first course

OCTOPUS, CRAB & BABY RED POTATO SALAD

What goes great with seafood is—more seafood! In this dish, we've combined tender octopus with crab in a salad made of barely cooked baby red potatoes, and tossed it with a smoky, salty dressing. The resulting blend of unctuous flavors and textures makes it hard to put the fork down. Ponzu is a Japanese sauce made of soy sauce infused with lemon juice, rice vinegar, and dried bonito flakes. Tangy and bright, it makes a wonderful dipping sauce for seafood.

> 1 pound baby red potatoes
>
> 1 sweet white onion, diced
>
> 3 tablespoons ponzu sauce
>
> 1 teaspoon salt
>
> 1 teaspoon freshly ground black pepper
>
> 1 fresh small octopus, or 8 ounces frozen or canned octopus, sliced
>
> 6 ounces fresh crabmeat (¾ cup)
>
> 2 garlic cloves, minced
>
> I bunch flat-leaf parsley, stemmed and minced
>
> 2 tablespoons minced fresh chives, plus more for garnish
>
> 4 tablespoons extra-virgin olive oil
>
> 2 tablespoons freshly squeezed lemon juice
>
> 1 tablespoon red pepper flakes

■ Scrub the baby potatoes, place them in a saucepan, and cover with 3 inches of water. Place over high heat and bring the water to a gentle simmer. Cook for 10 to 12 minutes, until soft. Drain and slice into quarters. In a small bowl, combine the potatoes and onion. Toss with the ponzu sauce, salt, and pepper. Set aside for about 10 minutes to let the flavors combine.

continued on page 55

- To prepare fresh octopus, make a circular cut around the beak and pull it gently toward you, removing the attached internal organs. Discard the ink sack and organs, and rinse the body cavity under running water. Bring a large pot of salted water to a boil. Carefully drop the octopus into the boiling water and cook for 30 to 45 minutes, until fork-tender. Remove the pot from the heat and let the octopus sit in the hot water for about 5 minutes to further tenderize the meat. Using tongs, transfer the octopus to a clean surface to drain and cool. When cooled enough to handle, use a sharp knife to cut the octopus into small slices.

- In a bowl, combine the crabmeat, octopus, garlic, parsley, and the 2 tablespoons chives. Add the olive oil and lemon juice and gently toss. Add the red pepper flakes and the potatoes and onions; toss to combine. Taste and adjust the seasoning.

- Arrange the salad on a large salad plate and garnish with chives. This salad can be made ahead of time and refrigerated for up to 24 hours without significant loss of flavor, but it tastes best when eaten within 2 hours of preparation.

Serves 4 as a first course

SMALL PLATES

SPICY CRAB SHOOTERS

As one of our recipe testers said: "This is a party in your mouth!" And indeed it is. These shooters may be small, but they pack a punch. Shooters make great party fare or a surprising amuse-bouche to kick off a dinner. Best of all, they can be prepared beforehand and refrigerated until party time. Line the shot glasses on a tray to place on a cocktail table, or carry them around the room to offer to your guests.

> 1 cup tomato juice
> 2 shots vodka
> 1 teaspoon grated fresh horseradish
> 2 teaspoons Worcestershire sauce
> 1 teaspoon Tabasco sauce
> 1 teaspoon honey
> 1 tablespoon freshly squeezed lime juice
> Freshly ground pepper
> 12 fresh Dungeness crab legs, cooked and shelled, or 8 ounces canned crab legs
> 1 tablespoon minced fresh chives

- Chill 12 shot glasses or small (3- to 4-ounce) glasses in the freezer for 15 to 30 minutes. In a blender or a cocktail shaker, combine the tomato juice, vodka, horseradish, Worcestershire sauce, Tabasco, honey, and lime juice. Blend for 30 seconds or shake vigorously to combine all the ingredients. Season with pepper. Refrigerate for 20 to 30 minutes to chill.

- Arrange the chilled glasses on a serving tray. Slide the crab legs onto cocktail skewers and place one in each glass. Divide the tomato cocktail among the glasses and garnish with a light sprinkling of chives. Serve immediately.

Serves 12 as an appetizer

CRAB PIZZA

WITH MOZZARELLA, CHERRY TOMATOES, AND BASIL

If you've never had crab pizza, you're in for a treat! Adorned with only a few excellent-quality ingredients, this pizza is a beautiful showcase for best-quality crabmeat. A word to the wise: This always disappears within minutes, so be sure to secure a slice for yourself before you set it on the table!

> ½ cup warm water (105° to 115°F)
> 1 package (2¼ teaspoons) active dry yeast
> 1 teaspoon sugar
> 1½ cups unbleached all-purpose flour
> 1 teaspoon salt
> 2 tablespoons cornmeal
> 2 tablespoons olive oil
> 6 ounces crabmeat (¾ cups)
> 16 to 20 cherry tomatoes, halved
> ¼ cup chopped green onion
> 6 ounces fresh mozzarella cheese
> 16 to 20 fresh basil leaves

- Pour the water into a small bowl and sprinkle the yeast and sugar over the top. Whisk or swirl to blend. Let stand until foamy, about 5 minutes. If the mixture doesn't foam, discard and start over with new yeast.

- In a large bowl, stir 1 cup of the flour and the salt together with a whisk. Add the yeast mixture and stir with a wooden spoon to blend. Stir in the remaining flour ¼ cup at a time, until the dough clings together in a ball.

- On a lightly floured work surface, knead the dough for 7 to 8 minutes, until smooth and elastic.

- Divide the dough into 2 pieces and form each into a ball. Place on a lightly oiled baking sheet and cover with a damp cloth. Let rise in a warm place until doubled in size, about 45 minutes. Punch down gently; the dough is now ready to be stretched into shape for the pizza.

- Preheat the oven to 375°F. Lightly oil two 9- to 11-inch pizza pans or ovenproof skillets and dust with the cornmeal. Shake the pans to evenly distribute the cornmeal. Place a ball of dough in the center of each pan and stretch lightly until they reach the edges and are fairly even in thickness. Drizzle with the olive oil and spread it around. Scatter the crabmeat, tomatoes, and green onions evenly over the doughs. Tear the cheese into coarse pieces and scatter it on top.

- Bake for 12 to 15 minutes, until the cheese is bubbly and melted and the crust is golden brown. Remove from the oven and scatter the basil leaves over the top. Cut into wedges and serve immediately.

Serves 4 to 6 as an appetizer or light snack

CRAB ROCKEFELLER

We've taken the famous New Orleans recipe for oysters Rockefeller and reinvented it with crab. In this delectable dish, crabmeat is laced with Pernod and cooked with butter and cheese inside a crab shell, making the presentation as dramatic as the dish is delicious. Since it is so rich, we recommend serving it as an appetizer, to be spread on thin slices of toasted sourdough.

8 ounces crabmeat (1 cup)

2 tablespoons finely chopped green onions

1 crab top shell, cleaned and dried (optional)

3 tablespoons unsalted butter, at room temperature

3 tablespoons finely chopped baby spinach leaves

1 tablespoon minced fresh tarragon

¼ cup panko (Japanese bread crumbs)

1 teaspoon Tabasco sauce

2 tablespoons Pernod or Herbsaint liqueur (optional)

½ cup shredded mild Cheddar cheese

1 tablespoon minced fresh flat-leaf parsley

Twelve thin slices sourdough bread, toasted

■ Preheat the oven to 350°F. In a small bowl, mix together the crabmeat and the green onions. Place the crab shell, if using, on a work surface and fill it with the crab mixture. Otherwise, place the crab mixture in a small gratin dish.

continued on page 64

- In a bowl, combine the butter, spinach, tarragon, bread crumbs, and Tabasco sauce. Mash with the back of a wooden spoon until thoroughly blended. Fold in the liqueur and half of the cheese. Spread over the crabmeat mixture. Top with the remaining cheese. Place the filled shell on a baking sheet and bake for 10 to 15 minutes, until the cheese is bubbly and golden brown.

- Remove from the oven and sprinkle with the parsley. Place the shell in the center of a serving platter and surround with the toasted bread. Serve immediately.

Serves 4 to 6 as an appetizer

CHILE-GLAZED CRAB LOLLIPOPS

WITH PINEAPPLE-HORSERADISH DIPPING SAUCE

These "lollipops" are a unique way to kick off your next party or special event. They're easy to make and downright addictive to eat. The chile glaze over the crunchy exterior imparts a sweet-hot punch, while the dipping sauce adds a creamy zing. They may be "grown-up" lollipops, but they're just as much fun to eat as the candy version!

3 cups chicken stock

2 tablespoons unsalted butter

1 cup Arborio rice

6 ounces crabmeat (¾ cup)

1 tablespoon Dijon mustard

2 tablespoons finely chopped green onions

Freshly ground black pepper

¾ cup all-purpose flour

2 egg whites, beaten just until foamy

1 cup panko (Japanese bread crumbs)

Canola oil for frying

¼ cup freshly squeezed orange juice

¼ cup granulated sugar

1 teaspoon red pepper flakes

½ teaspoon sea salt

3 tablespoons pineapple juice

1 tablespoon prepared horseradish

¼ cup sour cream

1 tablespoon packed brown sugar

continued on page 66

- In a saucepan, bring the stock to a low simmer. In another saucepan, melt the butter over medium heat. Add the rice and stir to coat the grains with butter. Sauté for 3 to 4 minutes, stirring, until the rice grains become translucent on the edges. Add ½ cup of the stock and stir until the rice has absorbed nearly all of the stock. Repeat with the remaining stock, ½ cup at a time, for a total of about 18 minutes, or until the rice is al dente and all the liquid is absorbed. Remove from the heat and let cool completely.

- Put the rice mixture in a bowl and stir in the crabmeat, mustard, and green onions. Season to taste with pepper.

- Pinch off lime-sized portions of the rice mixture and roll into 2-inch balls. Place the balls in a single layer on a sheet of waxed paper. Put the flour, egg whites, and panko into 3 separate shallow bowls. Moving quickly, roll the balls one by one in the flour, then dip them in the egg, then roll them in the bread crumbs until thoroughly coated. Place in a single layer on a sheet of waxed paper.

- In a large, heavy skillet, heat 1 to 2 inches oil over high heat to 375°F; it should be hot and bubbly. Fry the rice balls in batches, 4 or 5 at a time, for 3 to 4 minutes, until golden brown and crisp. Using a slotted spoon, transfer to paper towels to drain. Move to a platter and place in a low oven to keep warm until all of the lollipops are cooked.

- Pour the orange juice into a small, nonreactive skillet and place over medium-high heat. Add the granulated sugar and stir. The mixture will bubble as the sugars begin to caramelize. Add the pepper flakes and salt. Cook until reduced by half, about 4 minutes. Remove from the heat. Stick a wooden skewer about halfway through each rice ball to form a "lollipop" and arrange on a serving platter. Generously drizzle the glaze over the lollipops, allowing it to drip down the sides.

- To prepare the dipping sauce, combine the pineapple juice, horseradish, sour cream, and brown sugar in a small bowl, and whisk to blend. Transfer the sauce to a serving bowl and place on the serving tray with the lollipops. Serve at once.

Makes 25 to 30 lollipops

SMOKED SALMON, CRAB & AVOCADO BRUSCHETTA

Need a simple yet stunning starter for a luncheon or cocktail party? This is it. We've been known to duck into the kitchen and create a platter of these delicious morsels in mere minutes, and they're snapped up just as quickly. You could just as easily turn these ingredients into hearty sandwiches by piling the salmon, crab, and avocado into warm, crusty rolls.

6 thin slices sourdough or other good bread, crusts removed
4 tablespoons extra-virgin olive oil
6 ounces smoked salmon, thinly sliced
12 Dungeness crab legs, cooked and shelled, or 6 ounces jumbo lump crabmeat (¾ cup)
2 avocados, peeled, pitted, and cut into 12 thick slices
1 tablespoon basil-infused olive oil
Sea salt or kosher salt for sprinkling
Fresh basil leaves for garnish

- Preheat the broiler. Cut each slice of bread in half on the diagonal to form 2 triangles. Place the slices on a baking sheet and brush both sides with olive oil. Place under the broiler, 6 to 10 inches from the heat source, for 30 seconds, or until golden brown and crisp around the edges. Flip the bread over and toast the second side for 30 seconds, or until golden brown and crisp around the edges. Remove from the oven. Arrange on a serving platter. Lay 1 slice of salmon on each bread triangle and place 1 crab leg or a lump of crabmeat on top. Finish with a slice of avocado.

- When the bruschetta are all assembled, drizzle the basil-infused oil over the top. Sprinkle with salt. Garnish the platter with basil leaves and serve.

Serves 6 as an appetizer

CRAB BRANDADE

Brandade is traditionally made with potatoes and salt cod. Here, we've substituted crab, which is far easier to work with than salt cod, but makes a similarly dense, creamy dish. Brandade can be served as a side dish, but is best as an appetizer, spread on thin pieces of crostini.

> 5 to 7 cloves garlic, unpeeled
> 1/4 cup olive oil, plus 2 tablespoons
> 1 cup bottled clam juice
> 1/2 cup heavy cream
> 3 to 4 large russet potatoes, peeled and diced (2 cups)
> 1 pound crabmeat (2 cups)
> Salt and freshly ground pepper to taste
> 1 sweet or sourdough baguette, thinly sliced

■ Preheat the oven to 250°F. In an ovenproof skillet, combine the garlic and the 1/4 cup olive oil and cook over low heat for 25 minutes, stirring halfway through, until the cloves begin to soften. Place the skillet in the oven and bake for 25 to 30 minutes, until the cloves are golden brown and slightly wrinkled. Remove from the oven and set aside to cool. Increase the oven temperature to 325°F.

■ Meanwhile, combine the clam juice and cream in a large, heavy saucepan. Stir in the diced potatoes. Cook over medium heat for 35 to 40 minutes, stirring frequently, until the potatoes are soft and easily mashed with the back of a spoon. Remove from the heat.

■ Squeeze the roasted garlic from their skins and add to the potato mixture; discard the garlic skins. Using a potato masher, mash the potatoes to form a thick, creamy mixture. Stir in the crabmeat to combine thoroughly. Season with salt and pepper.

continued on page 70

- Using a rubber spatula, scrape the mixture into a buttered 4-cup gratin dish. Bake, uncovered, for 25 to 30 minutes, until golden brown and crisp.

- Preheat the broiler. Place the bread slices on a baking sheet. Brush with the remaining 2 tablespoons olive oil on one side and broil 6 to 10 inches from the heat source for 2 to 3 minutes, until golden brown. Turn the slices over and toast on the other side. Remove from the oven and let cool on a wire rack.

- Place the gratin dish on a large serving platter and arrange the crostini around the dish.

Serves 4 to 6 as an appetizer

FISHERMAN'S WHARF CRAB CAKES

WITH CUCUMBER SALAD AND BASIL AIOLI

Crab cakes are a featured item on nearly every menu on Fisherman's Wharf. In this recipe, we mix crabmeat with diced green onions and celery for crunch, then fry them until golden brown and crisp. As you enjoy your crab cakes at home, you'll almost be able to imagine that you're on the Wharf, watching the fishing boats and listening to the sea lions.

8 to 10 cloves roasted garlic (see page 69; optional)

3 large egg yolks

½ cup chopped fresh basil

1 teaspoon coarse sea salt or kosher salt

1½ lemons

¾ cup extra-virgin olive oil

1 English cucumber, peel intact, cut into thin slices

1 (4-ounce) can diced peeled green chiles

¼ cup diced red bell pepper

¼ cup rice wine vinegar

¼ cup light soy sauce

2 tablespoons toasted sesame oil

3 tablespoons sugar

1 teaspoon minced fresh ginger

1 tablespoon minced garlic, plus ¼ teaspoon

½ teaspoon red pepper flakes

12 ounces crabmeat (1½ cups)

1½ cups panko (Japanese bread crumbs), plus ¾ cup for coating

continued on page 73

⅓ cup finely chopped red bell pepper

⅓ cup finely chopped yellow bell pepper

⅓ cup finely chopped green bell pepper

⅓ cup diced celery

⅓ cup diced green onions

¾ cup mayonnaise

¼ cup minced fresh basil

1 tablespoon salt

1 tablespoon freshly ground black pepper

1 egg white, beaten just until foamy

½ cup all-purpose flour

Canola oil for deep-frying

Minced fresh chives for garnish

- To prepare the aioli, squeeze the garlic cloves to extract all of the roasted garlic. In a blender or food processor, combine the roasted garlic, egg yolks, ¼ cup of the chopped basil, sea salt, and juice from the ½ lemon (about 1 tablespoon). Pulse until smooth. With the machine running, gradually add the olive oil, first in drops, and then in a thin stream, and process until creamy and thick. Add the remaining ¼ cup chopped basil; pulse to incorporate. Use immediately, or cover and refrigerate for up to 3 days.

- To prepare the cucumber salad, combine the cucumber, chiles, and diced red bell pepper in a bowl. In a small bowl, whisk together the vinegar, soy sauce, sesame oil, sugar, ginger, the ¼ teaspoon minced garlic, and the red pepper flakes. Pour over the cucumber mixture and toss to combine. Let stand at room temperature for at least 15 to 20 minutes before serving, or store in the refrigerator for up to 3 hours. The longer the salad sits, the more flavorful the cucumbers become.

- In a large bowl, mix together the crabmeat, the 1½ cups panko, the finely chopped red, yellow, and green bell peppers, the celery, and the green onions. In a small bowl, whisk the mayonnaise together with the remaining 1 tablespoon minced garlic, the minced basil, the zest

continued on page 74

and juice from the remaining lemon, the salt, and the pepper. Fold the mayonnaise mixture into the crab mixture.

- Line a baking sheet with waxed paper. With dry hands, shape the crab mixture into 16 to 20 mounds for appetizers or 8 to 10 mounds for entrée servings. Gently form the mounds into patties.

- Line up 3 shallow bowls. Put the beaten egg white in one bowl, the flour in the second, and the remaining ¾ cup panko in the third. Dredge the crab cakes in the flour, tapping to remove the excess, then dip in the egg wash. Finally, roll them in the panko until fully coated on all sides.

- In a large, heavy skillet, heat 2 to 3 inches oil over high heat to 375°F; it should be hot and bubbly. Working in small batches, fry the crab cakes for 1 minute on each side, or until golden brown and crisp. Using a slotted spoon, transfer to paper towels to drain. Move to a baking dish and place in a low oven to keep warm until all the crab cakes are done.

- Serve the crab cakes with the cucumber salad on the side. The aioli can be served on top or in a bowl alongside for dipping. Garnish the crab cakes with a sprinkling of chopped chives.

Serves 8 to 10 as an appetizer or 4 to 6 as a light lunch

SIZZLING CRAB, MUSSELS & SHRIMP

WITH GARLIC BUTTER

One of the most satisfying ways to eat crab is to devour it straight from the shell. Here, we've heaped crab legs onto a large cast-iron griddle pan with mussels and shrimp, and roasted them on the stove top to create a tower of delectable seafood! We like the rectangular griddle pans from Lodge Skillets, which can be found at many kitchen stores or camping supply stores. They're made of heavy, durable cast iron, and they last for years. You can also use a cast-iron skillet or any skillet or pancake griddle if you don't have cast-iron versions handy.

> 3 tablespoons olive oil
> 1 teaspoon freshly grated lemon zest
> 4 teaspoons minced fresh flat-leaf parsley
> 1 teaspoon sea salt, plus more as needed
> 1 pound extra-large shrimp (16 to 20 per pound), in the shell
> 1½ pounds Dungeness or blue crab legs, in the shell
> 1 pound P.E.I. (Prince Edward Island) mussels
> Freshly ground black pepper
> 2 cloves garlic, minced
> 1 tablespoon small (nonpareil) capers
> 2 tablespoons dry white wine
> 4 tablespoons unsalted butter, at room temperature

■ In a large bowl, combine the olive oil, lemon zest, 2 teaspoons of the parsley, and the 1 teaspoon sea salt. Add the shrimp and toss to coat. Cover and refrigerate for 30 minutes to 1 hour.

continued on page 76

- Heat a large, cast-iron griddle pan or skillet over high heat for about 2 minutes, or until the surface is hot enough that a drop of water bounces and sizzles when sprinkled on it. Arrange the shrimp in a single layer in the center of the griddle of pan. Place the crab legs on one side of the shrimp and heap the mussels on the other side. Cook for 7 to 9 minutes, turning the shrimp once, until the shrimp are evenly pink and the mussel shells have opened.

- Remove from the heat. Discard any mussels that do not open. Sprinkle the mussels and crab legs generously with pepper and a little sea salt. Garnish with the remaining 2 teaspoons parsley.

- To prepare the garlic butter, combine the garlic, capers, wine, and butter in a small saucepan. Melt over low heat, stirring to combine the ingredients, and divide it between 2 ramekins. Place a ramekin at either end of the hot griddle pan or skillet.

- Bring the hot griddle pan directly to the table, placing it on a heavy trivet. Pass crab crackers, along with small shellfish forks or crab picks to extract the crabmeat and shellfish.

Serves 6 to 8 as an appetizer

CRAB-MANGO WONTONS

WITH SWEET CHILE SAUCE

Crab pairs beautifully with fruit, and here we've stuffed wonton wrappers with a mixture of crabmeat and cubes of ripe mango. The result is a crisp wonton that crunches when you bite into it, revealing a creamy, crabby center accented with sweet fruit. Served with the sweet-hot chile sauce, these are addictively tasty little bites. Ponzu is a Japanese sauce made of soy sauce infused with lemon juice, rice vinegar, and dried bonito flakes. Tangy and bright, it makes a wonderful dipping sauce for seafood.

2 tablespoons olive oil

3 red serrano chiles, seeded and minced

2 mangoes, peeled, pitted, and diced

1 tablespoon freshly squeezed lime juice

1 teaspoon sugar

2 teaspoons salt

10 ounces crabmeat (1¼ cups)

¼ cup mascarpone cheese

2 tablespoons minced fresh chives

1 tablespoon freshly squeezed lemon juice

1 tablespoon ponzu sauce

1 teaspoon freshly ground black pepper

1 package (4-inch) round pot sticker or wonton wrappers

Cornstarch if needed

Canola oil for deep-frying

continued on page 78

■ To prepare the chile sauce, heat the olive oil in a small skillet over medium heat until it begins to bubble. Add the chiles and cook for 2 to 3 minutes, until soft. Remove from the heat and let cool slightly. Pour into a small food processor or a small bowl. Add half of the mango, the lime juice, sugar, and 1 teaspoon of the salt. Pulse or mash to a thick, chunky sauce.

■ In a bowl, combine the crabmeat with the mascarpone, chives, lemon juice, and ponzu sauce. Toss to blend. Add the remaining mango, the remaining 1 teaspoon salt, and the pepper. Toss gently to blend.

■ Lay the wrappers on a work surface. Place 1 scant tablespoon of the crab mixture in the center of a wrapper and fold the edges up to form a triangle. Using a pastry brush or your fingertip dipped in water, lightly seal the edges. If the edges flap open, make a thin paste of cornstarch and water to use as the "glue." Be careful not to overfill, so the wontons don't burst. Continue until the wrappers are all filled, placing the filled ones in a single layer on a platter.

■ In a large, heavy skillet, heat 1 to 2 inches oil over high heat to 375°F; it should be hot and bubbly. Fry a few wontons at a time for 3 to 4 minutes, or until golden brown and crisp. Using a slotted spoon, transfer to paper towels to drain. Move to a dish and place in a low oven to keep warm until all of the wontons are cooked. Serve the hot wontons with the dipping sauce on the side.

Serves 6 to 10 as an appetizer

CRAB-CORN SOUFFLÉ

Most people think that soufflés are difficult to make, but in fact they're downright easy. This one requires only a few minutes of preparation; if you can remember not to open the oven door while it cooks, you'll have a gorgeous high-domed soufflé in no time. Go ahead: Bask in the oohs and ahhs that your guests will make when you bring it to the table. We'll never tell.

3 tablespoons unsalted butter

⅛ cup all-purpose flour

¼ teaspoon ground nutmeg

2 teaspoons salt

1½ teaspoons freshly ground black pepper

1½ cups milk

3 to 4 tablespoons finely grated Parmigiano-Reggiano cheese

2½ tablespoons minced shallots

½ cup fresh or frozen corn kernels

8 ounces crabmeat (1 cup)

½ cup shredded sharp Cheddar cheese

½ cup shredded mozzarella cheese

½ teaspoon red pepper flakes

6 large eggs, separated

■ Preheat the oven to 375°F.

■ Melt 2 tablespoons of the butter in a small saucepan over medium heat until it foams. Stir in the flour, nutmeg, and ½ teaspoon each of the salt and the pepper. Cook, stirring constantly, for 1 to 2 minutes, until the mixture is smooth and uniform. Gradually whisk in the milk in a slow, thin stream. Cook for 3 to 4 minutes, stirring occasionally, until thickened. Remove the béchamel sauce from the heat.

continued on page 80

- Generously butter one 8-cup soufflé dish or six 1-cup ramekins. Dust the inside with the grated cheese to create a light coating. Invert and tap lightly to remove excess.

- In a large skillet, melt the remaining 1 tablespoon butter over medium heat. Add the shallots and sauté for 3 to 4 minutes, until translucent. Stir in the corn kernels, crabmeat, béchamel sauce, Cheddar, mozzarella, pepper flakes, 1 teaspoon of the salt, and the remaining 1 teaspoon pepper. Stir with a wooden spoon to evenly combine the ingredients. Cook until the cheese has melted, about 4 minutes, stirring once or twice. Pour the mixture into a large bowl. Whisking constantly, add the egg yolks one by one and beat the mixture until light and frothy.

- In a large bowl, beat the egg whites and the remaining ½ teaspoon salt until stiff, glossy peaks form. Stir one-fourth of the egg whites into the crab mixture. Gently fold in one-third of the remaining whites at a time until blended. Pour into the soufflé dish, leaving ½ inch of space at the top to allow for expansion, or divide among the ramekins.

- Bake the ramekins for 20 to 25 minutes or the large soufflé dish for 30 to 35 minutes, until risen and golden brown. When you press the top with your finger, it should bounce back lightly, with a bit of wiggle in the middle. Do not open the oven door during the first 20 minutes of cooking, otherwise the soufflé(s) will fall.

- Bring the soufflé(s) directly to the table for maximum visual effect; serve immediately.

Serves 6 as a side dish

CRAB BEIGNETS

Beignets are small puffs of fried dough, often sprinkled with powdered sugar or coated with frosting. If you've ever visited New Orleans, you know that beignets with chicory coffee appear on the menus of many a New Orleans haunt. When they're fresh and piping hot, the crispy exterior shatters in your mouth to reveal a soft, creamy middle. We've created a recipe for savory beignets with crabmeat; with a light squeeze of lemon, these are little bites of heaven.

2 large egg yolks

3 tablespoons olive oil

Grated zest of 1 lemon, plus juice of 1/2 lemon

1 teaspoon minced garlic

8 ounces crabmeat (1 cup)

1 heaping tablespoon minced fresh basil

Salt and freshly ground black pepper

1/2 cup water

4 tablespoons unsalted butter, cut into bits

1/2 teaspoon salt

1/2 cup all-purpose flour

4 large eggs

Canola oil for deep-frying

2 tablespoons minced fresh flat-leaf parsley for garnish

Lemon wedges for serving

■ In a food processor or a blender, process the egg yolks for about 15 seconds, until light and fluffy. Gradually add the olive oil in a thin stream to create a thick sauce. Stir in the lemon zest and juice and the garlic, then fold in the crabmeat, basil, and salt and pepper to taste.

continued on page 82

- To make the beignet dough, in a saucepan, combine the water, butter, and salt in a saucepan. Bring to a boil over medium heat. Add the flour all at once and stir vigorously with a heavy wooden spoon so the mixture will form into a ball. Stir constantly, scraping the bottom of the pan to prevent the dough from burning, for 2 to 3 minutes more, or until the dough becomes golden brown and shiny, and a film forms on the bottom of the pan. Remove from the heat and transfer the dough to a bowl.

- Add 1 egg, beating vigorously to incorporate it thoroughly into the dough. Repeat to add the remaining 3 eggs, one by one, making sure that the previous egg has been fully mixed into the dough before adding the next. The dough should be glossy and viscous.

- Fold the crab mixture into the dough. Let cool, then cover and refrigerate for at least 45 minutes to 1 hour, or up to 3 days.

- To fry the beignets, remove the dough from the refrigerator. In a large, heavy skillet, heat 1 to 2 inches oil over high heat to 375°F; it should be hot and bubbly. Using a teaspoon or a melon baller, scoop the dough into 1-inch-diameter balls. Drop 5 to 7 at a time into the oil and fry for about 2 minutes, or until golden brown. Using a wire-mesh skimmer, transfer to paper towels to drain. Move to a shallow dish and place in a low oven to keep warm until all of the beignets are cooked. Sprinkle with the parsley and a light squeeze of lemon and serve immediately.

Serves 4 to 6 as an appetizer or light snack

LARGE PLATES

CRAB & CHEDDAR FRITTATA

If you've been searching for a breakfast dish that is simultaneously elegant and uncomplicated, look no further; with a preparation time of just minutes, this frittata will be ready to bring to the table in a jiffy. Slice it into thick wedges and serve with fresh fruit and yogurt alongside for a delicious meal. If you have any left over, which is quite unlikely, it tastes equally delicious at room temperature for a mid-morning snack or light lunch.

6 large eggs
¼ cup milk
1 teaspoon salt
1 teaspoon freshly ground black pepper
½ cup shredded white Cheddar cheese
6 ounces crabmeat (¾ cup)
¼ cup finely chopped Roma tomatoes
2 tablespoons minced fresh basil for garnish

- Preheat the broiler. Lightly oil a 6- or 7-inch ovenproof skillet and heat it over medium-high heat.

- In a bowl, whisk together the eggs, milk, salt, and pepper. Pour into the hot skillet and decrease the heat to medium. Cook for 1 minute, then sprinkle the shredded cheese, crabmeat, and tomato over the top. Cook for another 2 minutes, or until the edges just begin to set.

- Place the skillet under the broiler, 6 to 10 inches from the heat source, for 4 to 5 minutes, until the cheese is melted and bubbly and the edges of the eggs are firm. The eggs will keep cooking after you have removed the skillet from the broiler, so the center should be just slightly underdone.

- Remove from the broiler and gently slide the frittata from the skillet onto a warmed large plate. Garnish with basil and serve immediately.

Serves 3 to 4

CRAB BENEDICT

WITH ASPARAGUS AND MEYER LEMON HOLLANDAISE

Who was Benedict, and what inspired him to drizzle hollandaise sauce over eggs and toast? We can't answer that question, but we do know that this classic breakfast dish is even better with crab; the sweet, mild flavor of the crabmeat melds with the warm eggs and makes a perfect match with the lemony hollandaise. If you can't find Meyer lemons, which are sweeter than regular lemons, substitute a 2-to-1 mixture of lemon juice and orange juice.

½ cup (1 stick) unsalted butter, plus more for buttering muffins

2 large egg yolks

1 tablespoon fresh Meyer lemon juice

Salt and freshly ground pepper

2 tablespoons rice vinegar

1 teaspoon salt

4 large eggs

4 English muffins, split

8 Dungeness crab legs, cooked and shelled, or 6 ounces fresh crabmeat (¾ cup)

12 asparagus stalks, blanched and drained

4 lemon slices

2 tablespoons minced fresh flat-leaf parsley for garnish

Freshly grated nutmeg for dusting

■ To prepare the hollandaise sauce, melt the ½ cup butter in a small saucepan over low heat. Place the egg yolks in a double boiler over barely simmering water; whisk them for a moment until they are smooth but not fluffy. Gradually whisk in the melted butter in a slow, steady stream to make a smooth sauce. Cook for 2 minutes, stirring constantly. Turn off the heat but leave the sauce over the double boiler to keep warm. Stir in the lemon juice and the

continued on page 90

salt and pepper to taste. If the sauce thickens before using, thin it out with a tablespoon or two of hot (but not boiling) water.

■ Fill a large skillet with water to a depth of 2 inches. Place the skillet over high heat and bring to a simmer. Add the vinegar and salt. A flurry of bubbles should rise to the top of the water. As soon as the foaming subsides, working one at a time but quickly, crack an egg into a small bowl and gently slide the egg into the water. Cook until they reach desired doneness; for medium-set eggs, about 3 minutes. Remove the eggs with a slotted spoon. Lightly toast the muffins in a toaster until golden brown. Butter them generously.

■ Place 2 muffin halves on each warmed serving plate; place 2 crab legs or one-fourth of the crabmeat on one half. Place a poached egg on top of the crab. Drizzle with the hollandaise sauce. Arrange the second muffin half partially on top of the other, like a tilted cap. Place 3 asparagus stalks and a slice of lemon on each plate. Garnish with the parsley and a dusting of nutmeg. Serve immediately.

Serves 4

OPEN-FACED CRAB MELT

WITH AVOCADO AND SWISS CHEESE

Don't let the simple preparation of this sandwich fool you—it might be easy to make, but it is layered with luxurious flavors and textures: Creamy avocado, crunchy celery, and nutty Swiss cheese are all perfect partners for crab, and they elevate the humble sandwich into an exceptional dish.

4 miniature French baguettes or sandwich rolls, split and pressed open

2 tablespoons unsalted butter, melted

2 teaspoons sea salt

1 pound fresh crabmeat (2 cups)

¼ cup mayonnaise

1 tablespoon freshly squeezed lemon juice

¼ cup diced celery

½ red onion, sliced paper thin

1 cup shredded Swiss cheese

1 avocado, peeled, pitted, and sliced

■ Preheat the broiler. Lay the opened rolls on a baking sheet, cut side up. Brush with melted butter and sprinkle with salt. Lightly toast under the broiler, 6 to 10 inches from the heat source, for 3 to 4 minutes, until golden brown. Remove from the broiler, leaving the broiler on.

■ In a small bowl, gently mix together the crabmeat, mayonnaise, lemon juice, and celery. Divide among the baguettes, spreading the mixture evenly on both halves. Layer the sliced onion on top; sprinkle liberally with the cheese.

■ Place the sandwiches under the broiler again for 3 to 4 minutes, until the cheese is melted and bubbly. Remove from the broiler, top with the avocado slices, and serve immediately.

Makes 4 sandwiches

CRAB PASTA CARBONARA

The next time you're in the mood for decadence, reach for this recipe. The classic version of pasta carbonara is already rich with eggs and cheese—but we think there can never be too much of a good thing, and so we've added crab. The result is unqualified indulgence—a plush, creamy sauce studded with crab and pancetta and cradled in al dente pasta. Don't you deserve to go all out? Feeling a little French? Make your crab carbonara Saint-Germain style by adding 1 cup of frozen peas.

> 1½ pounds spaghetti pasta
> 6 ounces pancetta slices, finely chopped
> 3 tablespoons unsalted butter
> 4 tablespoons heavy cream
> 2 large eggs, beaten
> ½ cup freshly grated Parmigiano-Reggiano cheese, plus more for serving
> ¼ cup freshly grated pecorino cheese
> 8 ounces fresh crabmeat (1 cup)
> Salt and freshly ground black pepper

- In a large pot of salted boiling water, cook the spaghetti until al dente, 7 to 9 minutes. Drain, reserving 1 cup of the pasta water.

- In a large, heavy skillet, sauté the pancetta over medium-low heat for 4 to 5 minutes, or just until the fat begins to render. (High heat will make the pancetta rubbery and hard, so be careful not to overcook it.) Add the butter and cream; cook for another 3 to 4 minutes, stirring occasionally, or until the butter is melted. Remove from the heat.

- Add the spaghetti to the pancetta mixture, using tongs to thoroughly coat it with the sauce. Drizzle ½ cup of the reserved pasta water over the top; toss again. Decrease the heat to low and cook for 3 to 4 minutes, stirring several times, to let the sauce reduce slightly and heat the pasta.

- Crack the eggs over the pasta and quickly toss to combine, using the tongs. Stir in the ½ cup Parmigiano and the pecorino cheese until the eggs are cooked and the cheese is melted, about 3 minutes. Remove from the heat; add the crabmeat and season with salt and pepper to taste. If the spaghetti isn't moist enough, add another tablespoon or two of the reserved pasta water.

- Heap into warmed pasta bowls, and accompany with a pepper grinder and more grated Parmigiano cheese.

Serves 4 to 6

ANGEL HAIR CRAB LASAGNA

Lasagna has always been one of our favorite comfort foods, a dish we crave during the fall and winter. In this version, we've substituted angel hair pasta for lasagna noodles, and added cheese sauce and crab for a sumptuous dish that will make any occasion special. We like to pair it with a bottle of dry white wine—or, when we're feeling particularly festive, a bottle of bubbly.

12 angel hair pasta "nests," or 1¼ pounds angel hair pasta

¼ cup diced celery

¼ cup diced red bell pepper

½ cup finely chopped green onions

½ cup minced fresh basil, plus more for garnish

2½ cups heavy cream

1 tablespoon sea salt

1 tablespoon freshly ground black pepper

2 cups shredded fontina cheese

½ cup shredded mozzarella cheese

1 cup diced tomatoes

1 pound crabmeat (2 cups)

¼ cup shaved Parmigiano-Reggiano cheese, plus more for garnish

■ Preheat the oven to 325°F. In large pot of salted boiling water, cook the pasta until almost al dente, 1 to 2 minutes. Drain.

- In a large bowl, combine the celery, bell pepper, ¼ cup of the green onions, the ½ cup basil, the cream, salt, pepper, and shredded cheeses. Stir to combine. Add the pasta and stir gently until well blended. Stir in ½ cup of the tomatoes and ½ pound of the crabmeat. Transfer to a 9 by 13-inch baking pan. Scatter the remaining ½ cup tomatoes and ½ pound crabmeat over mixture. Top with the Parmigiano.

- Cover the pan with aluminum foil and bake for 1 hour. Remove the aluminum foil and bake for another 5 to 10 minutes, or just until the top turns golden brown. Remove from the oven and let stand for 10 minutes to set. Garnish with basil, shaved cheese, and the remaining ¼ cup green onions. Serve immediately.

Serves 6 to 8

CRAB FETTUCCINE ALL'AMATRICIANA

This pasta sauce is named for the city of Amatrice, located outside of Rome. The classic amatriciana uses guanciale, or salt-cured pork cheek, which is sautéed with thinly sliced onions and simmered gently with tomatoes and a pinch of red pepper flakes; we've added crab to make it that much more delicious. The pepper flakes can overwhelm the sweetness of the crab, so instead of adding it directly to the dish, we recommend that you pass a small dish of the flakes at the table so your guests can add them if they wish.

1½ pounds fettuccine pasta
2 tablespoons olive oil
1 yellow onion, very thinly sliced
⅓ cup diced guanciale or pancetta
1 pint cherry tomatoes, halved
1 tablespoon tomato paste
8 ounces crabmeat (1 cup)
½ cup grated pecorino cheese
1 to 2 tablespoons red pepper flakes

- In a large pot of salted boiling water, cook the pasta until al dente, 7 to 9 minutes. Drain, reserving ½ cup of the pasta water.

- Return the pasta to the pot and toss with 1 tablespoon of the olive oil to prevent the noodles from sticking together.

- In a skillet, heat the remaining 1 tablespoon olive oil over medium heat and sauté the onion for about 5 minutes, or until golden. Add the guanciale and sauté for another 5 minutes, or until it begins to crisp around the edges. Add the cherry tomatoes and toss. Cook for 3 to 4 more minutes, until the tomatoes become limp and glossy. Stir in the tomato paste.

- Pour the sauce into the pot with the noodles. Using tongs, quickly toss to coat the noodles. If the noodles aren't moist enough, add a tablespoon or two of the reserved pasta water. Add the crabmeat and toss again. Add more pasta water, if needed.

- Divide among warmed pasta bowls and sprinkle liberally with the pecorino. Pass the pepper flakes alongside.

Serves 4

PAPPARDELLE AL SUGO DE GRANCHIO

The title of this recipe translates as "pappardelle with a ragù of crab" and is made with a thick sauce of tomatoes, onions, carrots, olives, mushrooms, and crabmeat. The pasta isn't meant to be swimming in sauce; rather, the sauce flavors the pasta so that each bite is a blend of pasta, vegetables, and crab. We love serving this for a casual weekday dinner, with a green salad.

1 tablespoon unsalted butter

4 ounces cipollini or pearl onions

1 tablespoon balsamic vinegar

2 tablespoons dry red wine

1 pound Roma tomatoes, peeled (see page 31), seeded, and chopped

½ cup diced baby carrots

½ cup picholine or other green olives, pitted and coarsely chopped

2 ounces shiitake mushrooms, stemmed and chopped

½ cup chicken stock

Salt and freshly ground black pepper

1½ pounds pappardelle pasta

1 tablespoon olive oil

12 ounces crabmeat (1½ cups)

¼ cup diagonally sliced green onion

½ cup freshly grated Parmigiano-Reggiano cheese

1 tablespoon red pepper flakes

■ In a large, heavy skillet, melt the butter over medium heat and sauté the onions for 5 to 7 minutes, until softened. Add the balsamic vinegar and stir to coat the onions. Sauté for

continued on page 100

2 more minutes to caramelize the onions. Stir in the wine and cook, stirring, to scrape up the browned bits from the bottom of the pan.

■ Stir in the tomatoes, carrots, olives, and mushrooms. Sauté for 5 minutes, stirring frequently, until the carrots begin to soften. Add the chicken stock. Cover and simmer for 20 to 30 minutes to make a thick sauce. Season with salt and pepper.

■ In a large pot of salted boiling water, cook the pasta for 10 to 12 minutes, just until al dente. Drain and return to the pot, tossing with the olive oil to prevent the pasta from sticking together.

■ Gently stir the crabmeat and green onions into the hot sauce. Toss gently to combine. Divide the pasta among warmed serving bowls and ladle the sauce over. Sprinkle with grated Parmigiano and serve with the remaining cheese and pepper flakes alongside.

Serves 4

CRAB, BUTTERNUT SQUASH & ASIAGO RISOTTO

The velvety texture of this risotto is perfectly accented with sweet hunks of crabmeat and soft cubes of butternut squash. It makes an elegant dish for company, especially on a cold winter's night. Be sure to use the best-quality crabmeat that you can find; the larger the pieces, the better.

> 4½ to 5 cups chicken stock
> 2 tablespoons unsalted butter
> ½ cup finely chopped yellow onion
> ¾ cup diced peeled butternut squash
> 1¼ cups Arborio rice
> ½ cup dry white wine
> 2 teaspoons minced fresh thyme, plus more for garnish
> 1 teaspoon minced fresh rosemary
> 8 ounces fresh crabmeat (1 cup)
> ½ cup grated aged Asiago cheese, plus 2 tablespoons for garnish
> Salt and freshly ground black pepper

- Pour the chicken stock into a saucepan and bring to a simmer over medium-low heat.

- In a large, heavy saucepan, melt the butter over medium heat. Add the onion and sauté until softened, about 5 minutes. Add the squash and sauté for 5 minutes. Add the rice and stir until well coated with butter and beginning to turn translucent around the edges. Do not allow the rice to stick to the bottom of the pan.

continued on page 102

continued on page 102

- Add the wine and cook, stirring, until it has evaporated. Stir in the 2 teaspoons thyme, the rosemary, and 1 cup of the stock. Stir constantly until the rice has absorbed about half of the stock, then add another cup. Repeat until the squash is tender and the rice is al dente, 20 to 30 minutes. The risotto should be slightly soupy, not overly thick; the grains of rice should stick together, but not ball up.

- Remove from the heat and gently stir in the crab and the ½ cup grated cheese. Season with salt and pepper. Divide the risotto among warmed soup bowls. Garnish with the 2 tablespoons grated cheese and more thyme. Serve immediately.

Makes 4 servings

CRAB QUESADILLAS

When Andrea developed this recipe about ten years ago, he visited dozens of taquerias around San Francisco for inspiration. His goal was to capture the flavor of authentic taqueria quesadillas, packed with heat and flavor. The tomatillos are a key ingredient in this recipe; look for them at Latino markets or at farmers' markets.

1 pound tomatillos, husked and rinsed

1½ teaspoons salt

1 teaspoon freshly ground black pepper

4 tablespoons unsalted butter

½ yellow onion, chopped

1 (15-ounce) can crushed tomatoes, drained

1½ pounds fresh crabmeat (3 cups)

1 bunch green onions, chopped, including green parts

2 tablespoons sour cream

1 teaspoon ground cumin

1 teaspoon cayenne pepper

2 teaspoons red chile powder

4 (8-inch) flour tortillas

1 (7-ounce) can peeled whole green chiles

1 cup shredded yellow or white Cheddar cheese

½ cup sour cream

½ head romaine lettuce, sliced into thin strips

continued on page 105

- Preheat the oven to 200ºF with a baking sheet inside.

- In a large pot of salted boiling water, blanch the tomatillos for 3 to 4 minutes, until the skins appear tight and shiny. Drain. In a blender, puree the tomatillos until smooth. Season with 1 teaspoon each of the salt and pepper. Set aside.

- In a saucepan, melt 2 tablespoons of the butter over medium heat and sauté the onion for 3 minutes, or until translucent. Add the crushed tomatoes and the remaining $\frac{1}{2}$ teaspoon salt and simmer for 15 minutes, or until thickened. Set aside.

- In a small bowl, mix the crabmeat with half of the green onions, the sour cream, cumin, cayenne pepper, and chile powder.

- In a large, nonstick skillet, melt $\frac{1}{2}$ tablespoon of the butter over medium-high heat. Place a flour tortilla in the skillet and spread one-fourth of the crab mixture over half of the tortilla. Lay a green chile on top of the crab, then top with $\frac{1}{4}$ cup of the grated cheese. Fold the tortilla in half and cook for $1\frac{1}{2}$ to $2\frac{1}{2}$ minutes on each side, or until the tortilla is golden brown and the cheese is completely melted. Transfer to the baking sheet in the oven to keep warm while preparing the remaining quesadillas. (If you have a large, nonstick double-burner grill pan, you can prepare all 4 quesadillas at once.)

- Serve the quesadillas, whole or halved, with the tomatillo and tomato sauces over the top or on the sides. Top each quesadilla with one-fourth of the lettuce, sour cream, and remaining green onions.

Serves 4

GARLIC-ROASTED DUNGENESS "KILLER" CRAB

At Andrea's restaurants on Fisherman's Wharf, this is the most requested dish: enormous roasted Dungeness crabs in a peppery garlic sauce that will bring out the ravenous eater in anyone. You'll need to have a few crab crackers on the table, and plenty of warm finger towels handy for easy cleanup. Be sure to save the top shells to decorate the plate when you bring it to the table; this is one dish that looks as good as it tastes.

3 to 4 Dungeness crabs (2-plus pounds each), cooked and cleaned (crab butter reserved; see page 22)

½ cup dry white wine

3 tablespoons olive oil, plus more for brushing

2 tablespoons minced shallots

Leaves from 1 rosemary sprig, minced

1 teaspoon minced fresh thyme

2 tablespoons pink peppercorns

2 tablespoons canola oil

1 tablespoon sea salt, plus ½ teaspoon for sprinkling

8 to 10 roasted garlic cloves, mashed (see page 69)

Minced fresh flat-leaf parsley for garnish (optional)

- Place the crabs, claws down, in a baking dish. In a blender, process the reserved crab butter with ¼ cup of the wine until smooth and creamy. Set aside.

- Preheat the oven to 325°F. In a large, heavy saucepan, heat the 3 tablespoons olive oil over medium heat. Add the shallots, rosemary, thyme, and peppercorns and sauté for about

continued on page 108

3 minutes, or until the shallots are translucent. Stir in the remaining ¼ cup white wine, then the canola oil, the 1 tablespoon sea salt, and the crab-butter mixture. Decrease the heat to low and simmer, stirring occasionally, for 10 minutes, or until creamy and thick. Remove from the heat and skim any clumps from the top. Let cool for 3 to 4 minutes. Pass through a fine-meshed sieve into the saucepan. Add the mashed garlic cloves and stir well. Whisk until blended.

■ Generously ladle all but ¼ cup of the crab-butter sauce over the crabs and roast for 15 to 20 minutes, until the visible bits of crabmeat at the joint ends of the legs look slightly dry and crisp. Remove from the oven and arrange the crabs on a serving platter.

■ Sprinkle with the remaining ½ teaspoon sea salt, then place the top shells back on the crab bodies. Brush the shells with olive oil for a beautiful shine. Sprinkle the parsley over the whole platter and serve immediately, with the crab-butter sauce for dipping.

Serves 4 to 6

SAN FRANCISCO-STYLE SURF 'N' TURF

Who says you can't have your crab and your steak, too? We're partial to this combination of hoof and claw; a sumptuous filet with a side of crab legs just can't be beat. The next time you can't make up your mind—have it all!

1 tablespoon olive oil

6 (8-ounce) filet mignon steaks

1 teaspoon salt, plus more for seasoning

1 teaspoon freshly ground black pepper, plus more for seasoning

4 tablespoons unsalted butter

¼ cup dry red wine

2 pounds Dungeness crab legs, in the shell

2 tablespoons olive oil

1 garlic clove, minced

½ teaspoon grated lemon zest

■ Heat the olive oil in a large, cast-iron skillet or grill pan over high heat. Season the steaks with salt and pepper and place in the hot pan. Cook for 4 to 6 minutes on each side, turning once, for medium-rare. Transfer to warmed serving plates. Add the butter to the hot pan; when it sizzles, add the wine. Cook for 3 to 4 minutes, until reduced to a thick sauce. Drizzle the sauce over each steak.

continued on page 110

■ Meanwhile, toss the crab legs, olive oil, garlic, lemon zest, and remaining 1 teaspoon each of salt and pepper together in a large bowl. Heat a wok or large skillet over high heat and add the crab legs to the pan along with any liquid in the bowl. Using tongs, sauté until the legs are pink and the claws bright red, about 5 minutes.

■ Divide the crab legs among the serving plates, next to the steak. Serve with crab crackers, seafood forks or crab picks, and steak knives.

Serves 6

DRUNKEN CRAB ON SEAWEED NOODLES

Drunken crab hails from the Far East, and is made differently in each region of the vast Asian continent. In Singapore, cooks create a bisque with whiskey or brandy and add crabmeat just before serving. Here, we hew to a more Vietnamese-style method by steaming crab legs with whole peppercorns in dry white wine, and serving them over seaweed "noodles" sautéed in butter and more wine. Bottoms up!

1 tablespoon Szechuan peppercorns or pink peppercorns

1½ cups dry white wine

2 pounds Dungeness or blue crab legs, in the shell

1 package (10 to 12 sheets) dried seaweed sheets (not nori) or wakame strips

2 tablespoons unsalted butter

½ cup bottled clam juice

¼ cup black or white (or a combination of both) sesame seeds, plus more for garnish

Sea salt

1 lime, cut into 4 wedges for garnish

Chive blossoms for garnish (optional)

■ Heat a wok or a large, heavy skillet over high heat. Add the peppercorns and toast for 2 to 3 minutes, until slightly browned and fragrant. Add 1 cup of the white wine; bring to a boil. Add the crab legs and simmer for 4 to 5 minutes, until the legs are pink. Remove from the heat and set aside.

■ Place the seaweed sheets in a large bowl or baking dish. Add hot water to cover and soak for 10 to 15 minutes, until softened. They should be springy and wet and easy to bite into, like al dente pasta. Rinse and drain to remove any sand or dirt. Slice the sheets into ½-inch strips to create pappardelle pasta.

continued on page 113

- In a small skillet, melt the butter over medium-low heat. Add the remaining ½ cup wine and the clam juice and increase the heat to a simmer. Cook for about 5 minutes, then stir in half of the sesame seeds. Season with salt.

- Heap the seaweed into a large, shallow serving bowl and toss with the butter sauce. Arrange the crab legs on top and garnish with the remaining sesame seeds, the lime wedges, and the chive blossoms, if using.

Serves 4

FRANCISCAN

CRAB RESTAURANT

INDEX

MORE BOOKS FROM TEN SPEED PRESS

8" x 8", 184 PAGES, FULL COLOR
ISBN-13: 978-1-58008-686-8

8" x 8", 176 PAGES, FULL COLOR
ISBN-13: 978-1-58008-735-3

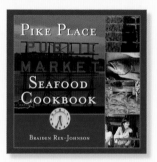

6¼" x 6¼", 144 PAGES, FULL COLOR
ISBN-13: 978-1-58008-680-6

Available from your local bookstore, or order direct from the publisher:
Ten Speed Press | www.tenspeed.com | 800-841-2665